ID0997194

His Land

WORD PUBLISHING

Word (UK) Ltd
Milton Keynes, England

WORD AUSTRALIA
Heathmont, Victoria, Australia
SUNDAY SCHOOL CENTRE WHOLESALE
Salt River, South Africa
ALBY COMMERCIAL ENTERPRISES PTE LTD
Balmoral Road, Singapore
CONCORDE DISTRIBUTORS LTD
Havelock North, New Zealand
CROSS (HK) CO
Hong Kong

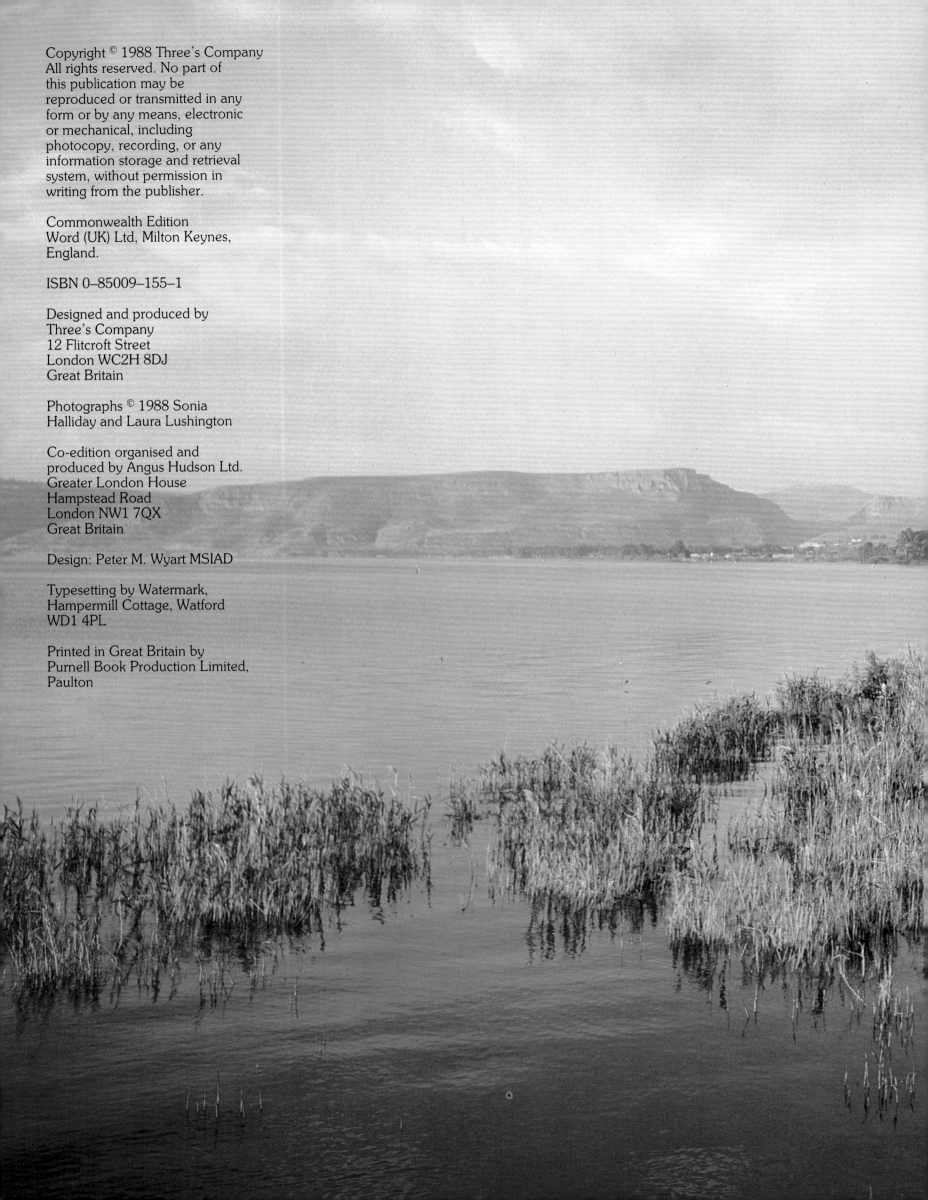

Copyright © 1988 Three's Company
All rights reserved. No part of
this publication may be
reproduced or transmitted in any
form or by any means, electronic
or mechanical, including
photocopy, recording, or any
information storage and retrieval
system, without permission in
writing from the publisher.

Commonwealth Edition
Word (UK) Ltd, Milton Keynes,
England.

ISBN 0–85009–155–1

Designed and produced by
Three's Company
12 Flitcroft Street
London WC2H 8DJ
Great Britain

Photographs © 1988 Sonia
Halliday and Laura Lushington

Co-edition organised and
produced by Angus Hudson Ltd.
Greater London House
Hampstead Road
London NW1 7QX
Great Britain

Design: Peter M. Wyart MSIAD

Typesetting by Watermark,
Hampermill Cottage, Watford
WD1 4PL

Printed in Great Britain by
Purnell Book Production Limited,
Paulton

His Land

A pictorial guide to places Jesus knew
Photographs by Sonia Halliday and Laura Lushington
Edited by Tim Dowley

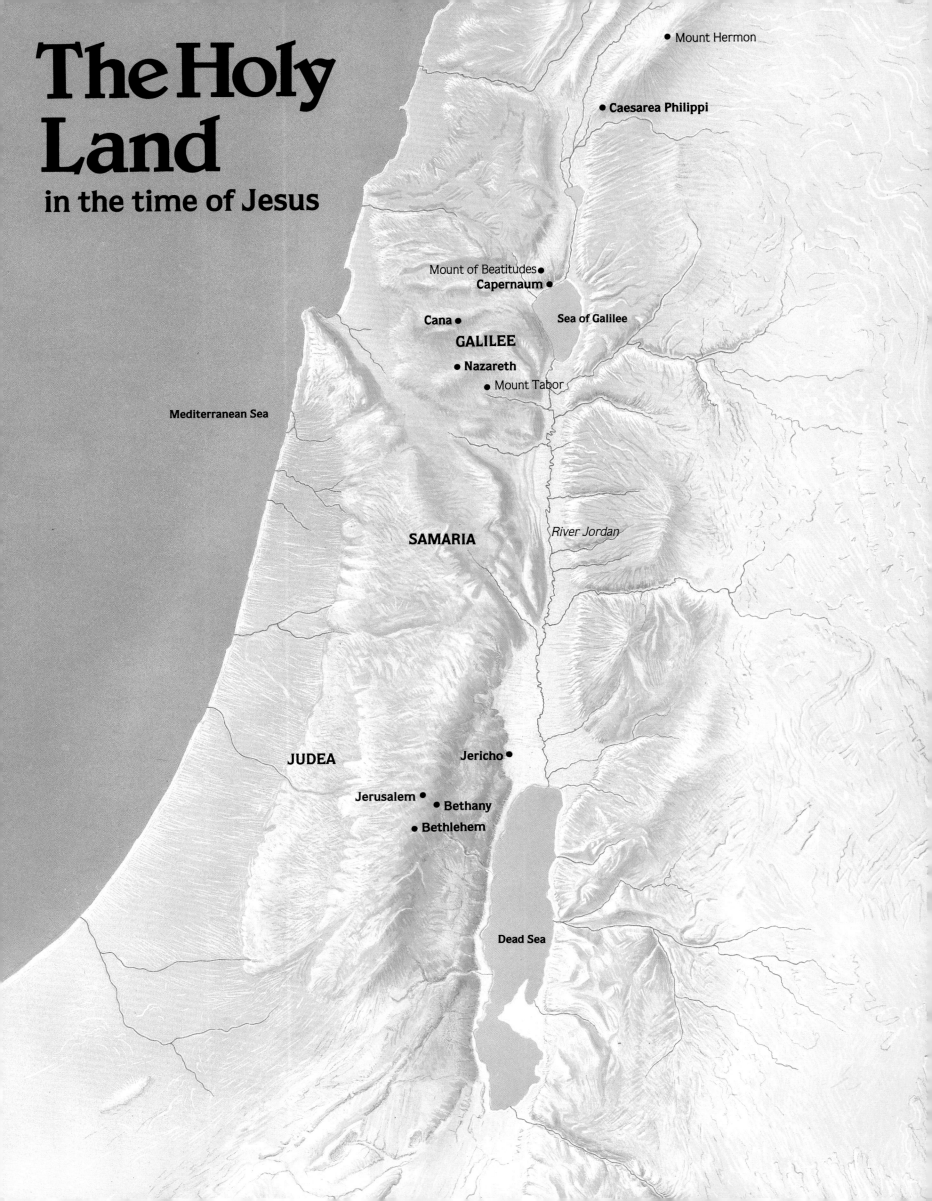

The Holy Land
in the time of Jesus

Mount Hermon

Caesarea Philippi

Mount of Beatitudes

Capernaum

Cana

GALILEE

Sea of Galilee

Nazareth

Mount Tabor

Mediterranean Sea

SAMARIA

River Jordan

JUDEA

Jericho

Jerusalem • Bethany

Bethlehem

Dead Sea

CONTENTS

Introduction	6
Prepare the way of the Lord	8
How Far is it to Bethlehem?	10
A Child is Born	12
The Church of the Nativity	14
Nazareth	18
The Visit	20
The Baptism	22
The Temptation	24
Galilee	26
Capernaum	28
The Mount of the Beatitudes	30
Lord of the Harvest	32
The Good Shepherd	34
The Sower	36
Mount Hermon	38
Mount Tabor	40
Living Water	42
Jericho	44
Bethany	46
Jerusalem	48
Palm Sunday	50
Gethsemane	52
Golgotha	54
Morning has Broken	56
The Empty Tomb	58
The Road to Emmaus	60
The Ascension	62
Index	64

Introduction

It is a great privilege for Christians to visit the Holy Land — His Land. Even today, when we are rapidly approaching the end of the twentieth century, it is possible for the visitor to imagine places as they were in Jesus' time. Much has remained unchanged in two millennia. The sower in his field; Galilee; the fishermen mending their nets; the hurly burly of the Jerusalem street market. Is it possible to sit beside the Sea of Galilee and be unaware of its history?

Once in a Lifetime

A visit to the Holy Land can prove to be one of the most memorable experiences in a Christian's life. We can see for ourselves the places we have read about so often in our Bibles; they take on a new reality, The names of towns, cities, rivers and mountains all take on new meaning for us.

This book has been created to remind the Christian visitor of that once in a lifetime experience. The pictures are exceptional, and have been chosen to bring out the resonances of the Gospel story. Accompanying these stunning pictures is a text which underlines the meaning of the great events of the story of Jesus' earthly life. We trace His steps from Bethlehem to Golgotha.

But this book will be equally valued by those unable to travel to Israel. It will enrich their understanding of the Bible and help them too to enter anew into the events of Jesus' earthly life.

Most modern visitors to the Holy Land travel from place to place by bus. But those who have the time and energy can travel the land on foot, using ancient tracks and pathways. They can enter more directly into the experience of ancient travellers; by covering the country on the ground they can gain a knowledge of the land which is beyond the grasp of the bus traveller.

Divine Conspiracy?

What sort of world was it into which Christ came? This is how the Christian writer J. Paterson Smyth put it:

'When Christ was coming, three races held the chief influence in the world — the Greek, the Roman and the Jew. The polished Greek, the powerful Roman, the hated and despised Jew. They were the prominent peoples of the civilised world . . . They *were* the civilised world. No others counted. Pilate recognized this when he put his inscription of the cross "in Hebrew and Greek and Latin."

'Now if these three peoples in the generation before Christ, without knowing or intending, seem almost as if conspiring together to prepare for His coming, is it too much to say that it at least suggests a divine preparation? Men who do not take

Christ into account may look on it as the chance happenings of history. But I think Christians, who recognize the stupendous thing about to come, will feel, as they read the history of the time, that not only John the Baptist but the world around was sent to "prepare the way of the Lord." At any rate, this is what happened.'

'Just like Him'!
And which way did God choose to come into the world? Listen again to Paterson Smyth:

'The first thing that strikes one — so utterly unlikely, so almost incredible at first sight — is the simple, ordinary way in which the great thing happened. If He had come with might, cataclysm and rending of the heavens, that was to be looked for. But to come in this simple, ordinary way! And yet, on second thought, is not this God's method in working all His wonders? Is it not "just like Him", as we say? . . . In the building of an oak, in the making of a planet, in the wonder of the dawn, in the miracle of the yellow harvest — that seems God's method always, quiet, simple, unnoticed.

'So Jesus came in utter, unexpected simplicity, not with pomp or rending of the heavens, but gently, quietly, as the dew comes or the dawn. Here is a stupendous happening, beyond the grasp of thought, and so easily does it blend with the simplest elements of life around that we feel some difficulty in retaining any wonder and awe. One feels almost as if reading an ordinary village chronicle.

A never ending story
'The story opens in a country village, secluded among the hills of Galilee. In the village street is a carpenter's shop and a country carpenter working at his bench with saw and hammer and chisel, making tables and chairs, and ploughs and cattle yokes for the countryside around. He is working hard and working happily, with the thought of his betrothal in his heart and of the home which he is preparing for his bride . . .

'Down the village his betrothed dwells, Mary, working in her home spinning and bread-making and drawing water from the well with the other village girls in the evening . . .'

Bedouin children lead camels to a water hole in the Negev desert.

Prepare the way of the Lord

'Behold, I send my messenger before thy
    face,
who shall prepare thy way;
the voice of one crying in the wilderness:
Prepare the way of the Lord,
make his paths straight —'

John the baptizer appeared in the
wilderness, preaching a baptism of
repentance for the forgiveness of sins. And
there went out to him all the country of
Judea, and all the people of Jerusalem;
and they were baptized by him in the river
Jordan, confessing their sins.
Mark 1: 2–5

Wind-swept trees in the Judean hills. It
was in wild countryside like this that John
the Baptist appeared preaching
repentance.

How Far is it to Bethlehem?

The sun is setting over the Bethlehem hills, touching the bare uplands of the wilderness of Judea and the purple mountains of Moab far off against the sky. On the valley road to Bethlehem is a straggling procession of travellers, and amongst them a young countrywoman, wearily riding, with her husband beside her leading the donkey. 'For there went out a decree from Caesar Augustus that all the world should be enrolled. And Joseph also went up from Galilee out of the city of Nazareth unto the city of David which is called Bethlehem, because he was of the house and lineage of David, to enrol himself with Mary, his betrothed wife, being great with child.'

A Bedouin woman with her baby stands outside her tent at sunrise, near Bethlehem.

So they draw near to Bethlehem through a land alive with historic memories. In the pastures beside them Ruth long ago gleaned in the fields of Boaz. In that hollow to the right outside the gates, brave men had died to bring David a drink of water from the Well of Bethlehem. A little off the road is a memorial sacred to all Jews, where the light of Jacob's life went out when 'Rachel died by me in the land of Canaan, and I buried her by the roadside on the way to Ephrath (which is Bethlehem).'

But their thoughts are preoccupied with greater things soon to come to pass. And Joseph is hastening to find rest and shelter for his companion. Those last miles have been very trying for her. At ordinary times there would be no anxiety about lodging, for in the friendly East hospitality is a sacred duty. But the travellers for the census have crowded the town. There is no room anywhere for the belated wayfarers, not even in the inn.

It was nobody's fault. Nobody knew Who was coming, except the adoring crowd looking down from the ramparts of the World from which He came, and they in that world of Goodwill would not blame us though they might well have enjoyed the unconscious irony of it all — the Lord of the Universe coming to this little world of His, and they have no room for Him.

A shepherd with his goats, near Bethlehem.

They were glad to take refuge at last in one of the natural caves in the hill-side where cattle were bedded. And there, with no kindly woman to aid her, came the pains of childbirth on that lonely woman, and 'she brought forth her son and wrapped him in swaddling clothes' — there was no one else to do it — and laid Him in the manger with the cattle around Him for His first infant sleep.
Did ever baby enter this world in lowlier guise? And do we not love Him the more for it?

A Child is Born

In those days Caesar Augustus issued a decree that a census should be taken of the entire Roman world. (This was the first census that took place while Quirinius was governor of Syria.) And everyone went to his own town to register.

So Joseph also went up from the town of Nazareth in Galilee to Judea, to Bethlehem the town of David, because he belonged to the house and line of David. He went there to register with Mary, who was pledged to be married to him and was expecting a child. While they were there, the time came for the baby to be born, and she gave birth to her firstborn, a son. She wrapped him in strips of cloth and placed him in a manger, because there was no room for them in the inn.

The shepherds and the angels

And there were shepherds living out in the fields near by, keeping watch over their flocks at night. An angel of the Lord appeared to them, and the glory of the Lord shone around them, and they were terrified. But the angel said to them, 'Do not be afraid. I bring you good news of great joy that will be for all the people. Today in the town of David a Saviour has been born to you; he is Christ the Lord. This will be a sign to you: You will find a baby wrapped in strips of cloth and lying in a manger.'

Suddenly a great company of the heavenly host appeared with the angel, praising God and saying,

'Glory to God in the highest,
and on earth peace to men
on whom his favour rests.'

When the angels had left them and gone into heaven, the shepherds said to one another, 'Let's go to Bethlehem and see this thing that has happened, which the Lord has told us about.'

So they hurried off and found Mary and Joseph, and the baby, who was lying in the manger. When they had seen him, they spread the word concerning what had been told them about this child, and all who heard it were amazed at what the shepherds said to them. But Mary treasured up all these things and pondered them in her heart. The shepherds returned, glorifying and praising God for all the things they had heard and seen, which were just as they had been told.
Luke 2:1–20

The visit of the Magi

After Jesus was born in Bethlehem in Judea, during the time of King Herod, Magi from the east came to Jerusalem and asked, 'Where is the one who has been born king of the Jews? We saw his star in the east and have come to worship him.'

When King Herod heard this he was disturbed, and all Jerusalem with him. When he had called together all the people's chief priests and teachers of the

Bethlehem at sunset. The towers of the Church of the Nativity can be seen on the skyline.

law, he asked them where the Christ was to be born. 'In Bethlehem in Judea,' they replied, 'for this is what the prophet has written:

"But you, Bethlehem, in the land of Judah,
   are by no means least among the
      rulers of Judah;
for out of you will come a ruler
   who will be the shepherd of my people
      Israel."'

Then Herod called the Magi secretly and found out from them the exact time the star had appeared. He sent them to Bethlehem and said, 'Go and make a careful search for the child. As soon as you find him, report to me, so that I too may go and worship him.'

After they had heard the king, they went on their way, and the star they had seen in the east went ahead of them until it stopped over the place where the child was. When they saw the star, they were overjoyed. On coming to the house, they saw the child with his mother Mary, and they bowed down and worshipped him. Then they opened their treasures and presented him with gifts of gold and of incense and of myrrh. And having been warned in a dream not to go back to Herod, they returned to their country by another route.

The escape to Egypt

When they had gone, an angel of the Lord appeared to Joseph in a dream. 'Get up,' he said, 'take the child and his mother and escape to Egypt. Stay there until I tell you, for Herod is going to search for the child to kill him.'

So he got up, took the child and his mother during the night and left for Egypt, where he stayed until the death of Herod.
Matthew 2: 1–15

The Church of the Nativity

Opposite: The sun reflects off the star on the bell tower of the Church of the Nativity, Bethlehem.

Bethlehem and the Church of the Nativity (left on the skyline) shortly after sunrise.

When Joseph, the carpenter from Nazareth (at the other end of Palestine) rode in to Bethlehem, as the Roman census edict commanded, the streets must have been busy enough. It suited the bureaucrats to have all the population return to their birthplace for the periodical enrolment and no provision was made for women like Mary, about to give birth to a child. One read the edict. One obeyed. We actually possess one such edict, dated a century later, and envisaging commisariat problems and difficulties in accommodation likely to emerge.

Where crowds gather in an eastern town the street sellers assemble. Bethlehem was a magnet for them. It was one of the land's most ancient towns, with a history as old as Jacob, who buried his beloved Rachel there, and those whose ancestry demanded their attendance were numerous. There were those of David's royal line, no longer great, and a host of other families. No wonder the inn was full.

THE EARLIEST CHURCH

The old doorways of the Church of the Nativity, first of Justinian and then of the Crusaders, were walled up, and the present small aperture made, to ensure that no desecration should come from crude invaders riding in. Anyway, it is salutary to bow on entering.

It is old, stained with history, gloomy inside. Through gaps in the present floor, the mosaics of antiquity are visible, perhaps the floor of the Empress Helena's first church on the site.

Down some steps is a cave, marble-faced, hung and cluttered with all the tinsel of men's devotions. How much better it would have been to leave unplastered with such integument the bare rock of the native earth.

THE PLACE OF NATIVITY

There is small doubt that this is truly the place of Christ's nativity. A chain of tradition can be traced back through Muslim to imperial times. There were, of course, two early gaps in the line. When the Romans closed in on Jerusalem in AD 70, the Christians had already fled to Pella across the Jordan. The war over, Jerusalem's ruins and the adjacent countryside would be occupied again and many a Christian would remember the sacred places.

The dark and cluttered cave beneath, rank with the smell of burning lamps, may well have been part of the famous inn. The terrain is given to such structures. A mile down the 'shepherds' fields' is to be seen a substantial cave, dry, and still in use...

NO ROOM IN THE INN

The innkeeper, of course, acted in no improper fashion. The nineteenth century travellers in Palestine found many such places — a higher platform where the guests could bed down on abundant floor where the animals were tethered. Joseph and Mary were not rich. The better accommodation in the inn may have been too expensive, and others of David's line, two eminent scholars, for example, who must have been there that night, perhaps preceded them and won priority.

The cave was warm and secure. Stone mangers, such as those dug up in the ruins of Megiddo by the archaeologists between the World Wars, must have been along the walls. One of them provided a crib. Perhaps somewhere it survives.

E.M. Blaiklock

A hurrying figure in traditional Arab costume in an old corner of Bethlehem.

Nazareth

The main features of the scene are little changed since His day. He, too, saw such narrow, crooked streets, and the houses outside among the fields and gardens, and the vineyards on the terraced hills, and the green valleys bright in the springtime with lily and larkspur and dog-rose and white anemone and all that profusion of rich and varied wild-flowers which makes one of the chief beauties of Northern Israel...

This is Nazareth, His home. In the carpenter's cottage in one of these streets He lived, a natural human boy in a natural human family... It needs an effort to pass from thinking of the Eternal Son, whose goings forth have been from of old, from everlasting, to thinking of and trying to visualize a little Boy in Nazareth going on messages for His mother and sweeping up the shavings in the carpenter's shop, to see Him among the children playing in the market-place the games of the unchanging child-world such as our children play to-day.

The Church of the Annunciation, Nazareth, the most impressive modern church in Israel. The fifth building to stand on this site, it was consecrated in March 1969. The church contains a series of fine contemporary stained glass windows.

19

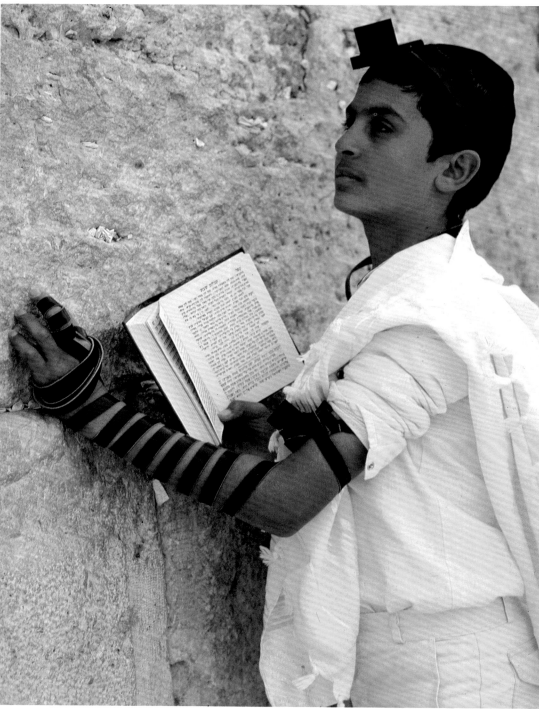

The Damascus Gate, one of the most impressive and busiest of the gates into the old city of Jerusalem. It was built by Suleiman the Magnificent in 1537, but stands on the site of a Roman gate built by the Emperor Hadrian in A.D. 135.

Inset Below: A Sephardic Jewish boy becomes a 'Son of the Law' at his Bar-Mitzvah at the Western Wall in Jerusalem. The ceremony is normally followed by a party for family and friends. After his Barmitzvah a Jewish boy is regarded as an adult.

The Visit

When Jesus was twelve years old comes the one recorded story of His youth, the only break in the long silence of thirty years... When a Jewish boy was twelve he became a 'Son of the Law'. His childhood was over. The serious responsibilities of religion came to him. And he could now go to the Festivals with the grown-up men.

So we read of Jesus that 'His parents went up every year to Jerusalem at the Feast of the Passover,' and when He was twelve years old 'He went up with them to the Feast.'

Bedouin on a track through the Judean Hills.

The Baptism

One day when the baptisms were over and John stood alone Jesus alone walked out to him into the water... And then — Jesus raised His eyes and looked him straight in the face. And then — he knew! — he knew! He whom he had dreamed of all those lonely years, straining his ears to catch the coming of His feet — the Messiah, the hope of Israel — He is come!

Can you imagine the tumult in the mind of the man, the astonishment, the prostrate humility, the sudden change of tone. A moment since he had been scathing imperiously the proudest of the Pharisees.

'Ye serpents, ye generation of vipers!' Now all his courage and confidence is gone — 'What! Thou! I have need to be baptized of Thee, and comest Thou to me?'

But Jesus gently bade him continue his office. True He had no need to be baptized into repentance. But this baptism was an initiating into the kingdom of faithful souls.

And Jesus would submit to it with the humblest of them all... John laid his hands on Him and bowed Him beneath the water. Thus was He initiated into His office. His private life closed. The new period opened. The humble villager from the workshop of Nazareth was henceforth the Messiah of God.

The River Jordan in the afternoon sun. South of the Sea of Galilee the Jordan has a very tortuous course. Though neither deep nor wide, Jordan is world renowned because of its significance for Christian believers.

The Temptation

'Then was Jesus led up into the wilderness to be tempted of the devil.' It is just after the Baptism. Then, we are told — immediately — the scene changes — in outward environment — in inward experience. From the Baptism to the Temptation. From Light to Darkness. Straight from the opened Heaven and the voice of the Father was Jesus led up into the wilderness to be tempted of the devil...

I see Jesus that day coming up out of the Jordan, His soul stirring with deepest emotions. He is passing through a supreme spiritual crisis. The Voice from Heaven, the Consecration of the Holy Ghost, the consciousness of supernatural powers, the beginning of His life enterprise, the realization of the tremendous thing it is going to mean 'to be about His Father's business.'

Its prominence in the Gospels makes it quite clear that this was no mere incident, but a solemn and most important crisis in the life of Jesus. It seems that He was meditating on His tremendous life-work, struggling with its perplexitites, seeking the way out, and that Satanic agencies of awful power were struggling with Him, trying to tempt, to mislead, to deflect Him from His course. He who became man to found the Kingdom of God must begin by encountering and defeating the powers of the Kingdom of Evil.

The Judean Hills at sunset. 25

Inset: An aerial view of Jericho, in the Jordan Rift Valley. In the foreground are luxuriant citrus groves, characteristic of this ancient oasis city; in the background, the Mount of the Temptation, by tradition the place where Jesus fasted for forty days. The Greek Orthodox monastery can be seen on the side of the mountain.

Galilee

See a very deep, central valley cutting Palestine from north to south, through which the river Jordan flows. Down in this deep valley near its beginning in Galilee, down at the base of the mountains, down deep, six hundred and eighty feet below the level of the ocean, with the land beside it rising in cliffs and terraces, lies the Galilean lake. Quite a little lake, about twelve miles by six. It is hard to realize that around that little lake was staged the central story of humanity...

In the days Jesus knew it Galilee was a very beautiful place. In the lands now bare of trees were beautiful woods. Where marshes are now there were noble gardens. Where a few wretched ruined villages stand today was a fringe of prosperous towns bordering the lake... Then there was a busy fishing fleet and king's barges and crowds of pleasure boats from royal Tiberias and the lake towns.

There was a very prosperous fishing trade. The lake fish had a high reputation in Jerusalem and the Syrian towns, and even as far off as Rome. Vegetation around the lake was so brilliant that it was almost looked on as a miracle. For nature, says Josephus, collected here the plants of every clime. Down by the hot lake shore grew tropical fruits, and terrace by terrace, ascending, gave the trees of many climates bearing fruit and flowers for ten months of the year. Jehovah, said the rabbis, created seven seas, but the Sea of Galilee was His delight.

An Israeli fisherman lifts his net on the Sea of Galilee in the early morning. Today fishing has once more become an important occupation on the lake.

Fishermen out early in their boat on the Sea of Galilee.

Capernaum

Right: A stone relief of the seven-branched lampstand, or menorah, ramshorn trumpet, or shofar, and incense shovel, from the third-century synagogue at Capernaum.

Opposite: Ruins of the third-century synagogue at Capernaum. Beneath this building have been found the remains of an earlier synagogue built in black basalt which may be the synagogue Jesus knew.

Sea

right where the broad
the Way of the Sea,

The Mount of the Beatitudes

The Beatitudes

Now when he saw the crowds, he went up on a mountainside and sat down. His disciples came to him, and he began to teach them, saying:
'Blessed are the poor in spirit,
for theirs is the kingdom of heaven.
Blessed are those who mourn,
for they will be comforted.
Blessed are the meek,

for they will inherit the earth.
Blessed are those who hunger and thirst
for righteousness,
for they will be filled.
Blessed are the merciful,
for they will be shown mercy.
Blessed are the pure in heart,
for they will see God.
Blessed are the peacemakers,
for they will be called sons of God.

Blessed are those who are persecuted
because of righteousness,
for theirs is the kingdom of heaven.
'Blessed are you when people insult you, persecute you and falsely say all kinds of evil against you because of me. Rejoice and be glad, because great is your reward in heaven, for in the same way they persecuted the prophets who were before you.

Salt and Light

'You are the salt of the earth. But if the salt loses its saltiness, how can it be made salty again? It is no longer good for anything, except to be thrown out and trampled by men.

Inset: 'Why do you worry about clothes? See how the lilies of the field grow. They do not labour or spin. Yet I tell you that not even Solomon in all his splendour was dressed like one of these.'
Matthew 6: 28–29

'You are the light of the world. A city on a hill cannot be hidden. Neither do people light a lamp and put it under a bowl. Instead they put it on its stand, and it gives light to everyone in the house. In the same way, let your light shine before men, that they may see your good deeds and praise your Father in heaven.'.

Prayer

'This is how you should pray:
  "Our Father in heaven,
  hallowed be your name,
  your kingdom come,
  your will be done
    on earth as it is in heaven.
  Give us today our daily bread.
  Forgive us our debts,
    as we also have forgiven our debtors.
  And lead us not into temptation,
    but deliver us from the evil one."'

Matthew 5: 1–16; 6: 9–13

The Church of the Beatitudes, built in 1937, stands on the Mount of Beatitudes, by tradition the place where Jesus delivered the Sermon on the Mount. The arches of this elegant building were made of white stone from Nazareth, the rest of the building of local black basalt. From the arcade visitors have a superb view over the Sea of Galilee.

Lord of the Harvest

The Franciscan Church of the Primacy, Tabgha, on the edge of the Sea of Galilee. By tradition Tabgha was the desert place where Jesus miraculously multiplied the five loaves and two fish to feed the vast crowd.

Inset: Mosaic of loaves and fish from the floor of the Church of the Miracle of the Loaves and Fishes, Tabgha. This is only part of a more extensive Byzantine mosaic now incorporated into the church completed by the Benedictines in 1981.

Jesus had taken His Twelve across the Sea of Galilee for a rest. But they had scarce landed when the crowd was upon them. His plan for a quiet holiday was defeated. How pleasantly He took it! These thousands of people intruding on His solitude, thwarting His purpose. But they wanted Him, wanted Him badly. That is always enough for Jesus. Those mothers with the sick children went to His heart. So He received them graciously and told them delightful things about the Fatherhood of God, 'and healed those that had need of healing.'

So passed long hours of strain and effort. Then the evening was come. And

Jesus was thinking of those tired, hungry people. And surely thinking also of the instruction of His Twelve. How far already had they learned to trust Him? So He turns to Philip. He sets Philip thinking. 'Where shall we get bread, Philip, that these may eat?' This He said to prove him. But Philip does not rise to the proof. 'It cannot be done, Master. It would take two hundred shillings' worth of bread.' 'Give ye them to eat.'

Jesus does not argue with him. He knows when to be silent. He lets the thought sink in. He will see by and by how the others will respond. But they are no better. When the day began to wear away they came to Him. 'Master, send them away, the day is far spent. Let them start for the villages and get something to eat.' Jesus said, 'Give ye them to eat.' 'Lord, how could we do it? Shall we buy in this desert two hundred shillings' worth of bread?' Evidently Philip had been talking.

Then Jesus proceeded to act. Great was the deed of kindness to the hungry multitude. Greater still in its far-reaching effects the lesson to the twelve men of still imperfect faith. 'How many loaves have ye? Go and see.' And they told Him they had only five loaves and two fishes, their own little supper. So He directed that the people should sit down in companies on the green grass in hundreds and fifties. 'And He took the five loaves and two fishes, and looking up to Heaven He blessed and brake and gave to the disciples to set before them...'

All four Evangelists tell of this miracle. The Twelve saw it. The multitudes saw it. We simply receive it as recorded. We believe in simple faith that it was wrought by His power who, as Lord of the Harvest, does a similar and greater miracle every year of our lives, multiplying for us each little grain of wheat thirtyfold, sixtyfold, an hundredfold.

The Good Shepherd

Judea offers as good ground as there is in the East for observing the grandeur of the shepherd's character. On the boundless Eastern pasture, so different from the narrow meadows and dyked hillsides with which we are familiar, the shepherd is indispensable. With us sheep are often left to themselves; I do not remember to have seen in the East a flock without a shepherd. In such a landscape as Judea, where a day's pasture is thinly scattered over an unfenced tract, covered with delusive paths, still frequented by wild beasts, and rolling into the desert, the man and his character are indispensable. On some high moor, across which at night hyenas howl, when you meet him, sleepless, far-sighted, weather-beaten, armed, leaning on his staff, and looking out over his scattered sheep, every one of them on his heart, you understand why the shepherd of Judea sprang to the front in his people's history; why they gave his name to their king, and made him the symbol of Providence; why Christ took him as the type of self-sacrifice.

The founder of Israel's one dynasty, and the first of its literary prophets, were 'taken from following the flocks'. The king and every leader of men was called a shepherd. God was the Shepherd of His people, and they the sheep of His pasture. In Judea Christ called Himself the Good Shepherd, and in Judea, taking another feature of her life, He said He was the True Vine.

'I know Mine own.'
Sometimes we enjoyed our noonday rest beside one of those Judean wells, to which three or four shepherds come down with their flocks. The flocks mixed with each other, and we wondered how each shepherd would get his own again. But after the watering and the playing were over, the shepherds one by one went up different sides of the valley, and each called out his peculiar call; and the sheep of each drew out of the crowd to their own shepherd, and the flocks passed as orderly as they came. 'The shepherd of the sheep, when he puts forth his own sheep, he goes before them, and the sheep follow him, for they know his voice, and a stranger they will not follow. I am the Good Shepherd, and know Mine own, and am known of Mine.' These words our Lord spake in Judea.

George Adam Smith

A shepherd with a mixed flock of sheep and goats in the Negev, southern Israel.

Inset right: An Arab shepherd carries a kid on his shoulders. The shepherd's life was rough and exhausting in Bible times. The lambs, unlike their stained-glass likenesses, could be heavy and dirty.

The Sower

'A farmer went out to sow his seed. As he was scattering the seed, some fell along the path, and the birds came and ate it up. Some fell on rocky places, where it did not have much soil. It sprang up quickly, because the soil was shallow. But when the sun came up, the plants were scorched, and they withered because they had no root. Other seed fell among thorns, which grew up and

choked the plants. Still other seed fell on good soil, where it produced a crop — a hundred, sixty or thirty times what was sown.'
Matthew 13:3—8

An Arab farmer at seedtime in his field near Samaria.

Mount Hermon

Away in Northern Galilee at the sources of the Jordan in the magnificent scenery at the base of Mount Hermon lies the beautiful little city of Caesarea Philippi. Somewhere there, in one of the mountain gorges above the town, He is retired with the Apostles. St Luke says He was apart from them alone in prayer. As He rises from His prayer He comes across to the little group.

'Tell me, what do the people think about Me? Who do they say that I am?'

'Master, some, like King Herod, think that You are John the Baptist risen. Some say You are Elijah come back to earth — some that You are Jeremiah, or one of the old prophets.'

'Who say ye that I am?'

Doubtless He knew very well what people thought and only asked with a further purpose in view. Suddenly He sprung the question direct upon them.

'But who say ye that I am?'

That was what really mattered. He was leaving His Kingdom of God in their care. How much had they learned or even conjectured from these two years of teaching and familiar intercourse? Prompt and unhesitating, Peter speaks for them all. 'Thou art the Christ, the Son of the living God!'

Snow-capped for much of the year, Mount Hermon dwarfs all other peaks in the vicinity. Its summit, at a height of 9,000 feet (2,800 metres) is in Syria, but its lower southern slopes are in Israel.

Inset: Niches in the cliff-face at Banias, biblical Caesarea Philippi. The arched niches once housed statues of the god Pan, whose cult was celebrated here in Roman times.

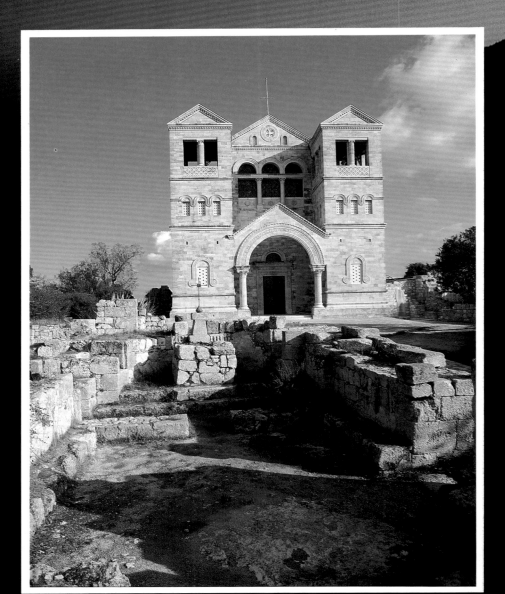

Living Water

When a Samaritan woman came to draw water, Jesus said to her, 'Will you give me a drink?'...

The Samaritan woman said to him, 'You are a Jew and I am a Samaritan woman. How can you ask me for a drink?' (For Jews do not associate with Samaritans.)

Jesus answered her, 'If you knew the gift of God and who it is that asks you for a drink, you would have asked him and he would have given you living water.'

'Sir,' the woman said, 'you have nothing to draw with and the well is deep. Where can you get this living water? Are you greater than our father Jacob, who gave us the well and drank from it himself, as did also his sons and his flocks and herds?'

Jesus answered, 'Everyone who drinks this water will be thirsty again, but whoever drinks the water I give him will never thirst. Indeed, the water I gave him will become in him a spring of water welling up to eternal life.'

John 4: 7–14

Jericho

The pilgrim crowd from the North is approaching Jericho and the townspeople are crowding through the gates to meet them. For the rumour has got abroad that Jesus, who raised Lazarus of Bethany from the dead, is amongst them who, men say, is coming, the Messiah of God, to deliver Israel from the Roman yoke. Their enthusiastic reception testifies to His hold on the people...

In the crush of the multitude, amid the shouts and acclamations, a blind beggarman is almost trampled down at the gate.

'What does it mean?' he asks, and the passers-by answer with a joyous shout,

'Jesus of Nazareth passeth by!'

And in a moment a wild hope is in the blind man's heart. Jesus, who healed that blind man in Jerusalem! Jesus is passing! Jesus is escaping him! Like a drowning man with his last hope slipping from him he puts his whole soul into that desperate cry. Even above the uproar Jesus heard it:

'Jesus! Thou Son of David, have mercy on me!'

Again and again rang out the passionate appeal by the name which the multitudes loved to call Him. The people tried to silence him, but no one could silence him. 'Thou Son of David, Thou Son of David, have mercy on me!'

And the compassionate heart of Jesus went out to him, as it must always to him or to you or to me when we sorely want Him. No shouting of multitudes can prevent His hearing. He stopped the whole procession on the spot.

'Call him,' He said.

And friendly people came to the blind man.

'Bartimaeus, be of good cheer! Arise! He is calling thee!'

He flung off his old robe. They led him trembling to Jesus.

'What wilt thou, My son, that I should do unto thee?'

'O Rabboni, that I may receive my sight!'

And immediately he received his sight and followed Jesus in the way.

Jericho was once held to be the world's most ancient city. The earliest occupation level discovered by archaeologists dates back to about 8000 B.C. This view shows the cultivated valley west of Jericho.

Inset Below Left: An Arab in traditional dress sits by the roadside.

Bethany

The sun rises over the village of Bethany (El-Azariye), on the eastern slopes of the Mount of Olives. Bethany is the last stopping place before Jerusalem on the road from Jericho. Beyond can be seen the hills of the Judean desert.

Inset: The reputed tomb of Lazarus in Bethany. The tomb itself is through the manhole leading from this antichamber.

Twelve miles up the wild hill road between Jericho and Jerusalem where the traveller in the parable 'fell among thieves,' and the pilgrim procession is passing by Bethany through rows of Bethany villagers crowded on the roadside to see Jesus of Nazareth, who had raised Lazarus from the dead. As they see in the crowd the eager faces of the Bethany family come to welcome them, Jesus and His comrades drop out of the procession, which continues its way to Jerusalem. This is on Friday, 'six days before the Passover.'

A FEAST

Next evening, when the Sabbath is over, there is a banquet in Bethany in honour of Him who had brought Lazarus from the grave, and, as we should expect, 'Martha served and Lazarus was one of them that sat at meat.' And Mary is in her little room unwrapping a precious alabaster vase, and her face is white with unutterable pain, for she more than others is in the secrets of the Master, and her woman's heart has divined that He is come to Jerusalem to die. The twelve Apostles are present. Amongst them take special note of one, not prominent before, that red-haired man of moody, sullen face who shall win undying infamy ere the week is out.

Irritable, disillusioned, disappointed, with evil purposes already forming in his heart, he is utterly out of sympathy with that company. For the moment he hates them all, and would vent his ill-humour on them.

A COSTLY GIFT

When Mary, in her uncalculating extravagance of affection, pours her costly gift over the Master's feet, he can see nothing in it beautiful or touching. It is a stupid, foolish extravagance. 'It might have been sold for three hundred pence and given to the poor.' In his ill-temper he would reprove indirectly even the Master who permitted this. The soul of Judas is in black mood this night...

Next morning all Bethany awoke in pleasant excitement, conscious that their village was the centre of observation. For they were housing Jesus of Nazareth, the prophet of God who had raised their townsman Lazarus from the dead, who, men said, was come as the Liberator of Israel. All the long pilgrim caravans turned to gaze as they passed. The Passover tents on the hill-side were pouring crowds into the village. The whole countryside was astir. Even the sightseers from Jerusalem were already crowding in. Bethany in a night had become famous.

Overleaf: Aerial view of the Temple Mount area of the old city of Jerusalem. The Dome of the Rock can be seen in the centre of the Temple Mount; immediately below it is the Western Wall, where the Orthodox Jews come to pray. The Dome of the Rock is sited over the area where once stood Herod's Temple, known so well to Jesus. On the right hand side, middle distance, is the Garden of Gethsemane, on the lower slopes of the Mount of Olives

Palm Sunday

Ride on, ride on in majesty! Hark, all the tribes hosanna cry.
O Saviour meek, pursue Thy road
With palms and scattered garments strowed.

The Dome of the Rock, the magnificent Islamic Mosque built on the site of Herod's Temple, Jerusalem.

Opposite: The Palm Sunday procession descends from the Mount of Olives towards the old city of Jerusalem. The Dome of the Rock can be seen in the distance.

So in humble pageant He rides in from Bethany, and His followers, as in a dream, march exultant beside Him, swelling with pride at the popular enthusiasm. The road is lined with crowds as for a royal procession. A shouting multitude is before Him and following. Now a larger crowd from the city swarms out to escort Him, telling each other of the raising of Lazarus. Every moment the enthusiasm increases. The common road is not good enough for His progress. The Galileans are carpeting the way with their garments. The multitudes are strewing His path with green boughs and the applauding shouts are audible in Jerusalem itself! 'Hosanna! Hosannna! Hosanna to the Son of David! Blessed is the King of Israel who cometh in the name of the Lord. Hosanna in the highest!...'

Sorrow over Jerusalem

Now the road turns suddenly to the northward, and here at this angle the city which had been hidden by the shoulder of the mountain bursts suddenly in all its glory on the view. The dream city of the Jew. The city of God. The centre of national memories. 'Jerusalem, the joy of the whole earth.' No other sight could so stir the heart of a Jew. And His heart is deeply stirred, but with sorrow and pain, that He could not have saved His nation and their glorious city from its doom. Oh, if they who had been born to the highest destiny on earth had but received Him, sent from God to them to accomplish their destiny! What a future there might have been for Israel and its lovely city, the centre of the spiritual empire of the world!...

The stones would cry out

The procession moved happily on unknowing. The acclamations were redoubled. 'Master,' cried some angry Pharisees in the crowd, 'rebuke Thy disciples.' 'Nay,' said Jesus, 'if these should hold their peace the very stones would cry out.'

As the tumultuous crowd swept in through the gates the foreign pilgrims came running to ask what it meant, and the answer of the multitude rang back like a triumphal chant: 'This is Jesus, the prophet of Nazareth of Galilee!'

Gethsemane

Jesus is arrested

When he had finished praying, Jesus left with his disciples and crossed the Kidron Valley. On the other side there was an olive grove, and he and his disciples went into it.

Now Judas, who betrayed him, knew the place, because Jesus had often met there with his disciples. So Judas came to the grove, guiding a detachment of soldiers and some officials from the chief priests and Pharisees. They were carrying torches, lanterns and weapons.

Jesus, knowing all that was going to happen to him, went out and asked them, 'Who is it you want?'

'Jesus of Nazareth,' they replied.

'I am he,' Jesus said.

John 18: 1–5

An ancient stepped road near the church of St Peter in Gallicantu, on the slopes of Mount Zion, Jerusalem. It is possible that Jesus and His disciples trod this road on their way from the Last Supper in the Upper Room to the Garden of Gethsemane.

Below: An ancient olive tree in the garden of Gethseınane, Jerusalem. In the garden stands the Franciscan Church of All Nations.

Golgotha

So the soldiers took charge of Jesus. Carrying his own cross, he went out to The Place of the Skull (which in Aramaic is called Golgotha). Here they crucified him, and with him two others – one on each side and Jesus in the middle.

Pilate had a notice prepared and fastened to the cross. It read, JESUS OF NAZARETH, THE KING OF THE JEWS. Many of the Jews read this sign, for the place where Jesus was crucified was near the city, and the sign was written in Aramaic, Latin and Greek. The chief priests of the Jews protested to Pilate, 'Do not write "The King of the Jews," but that this man claimed to be king of the Jews.'

Pilate answered, 'What I have written, I have written.'

When the soldiers crucified Jesus, they took his clothes, dividing them into four shares, one for each of them, with the undergarment remaining. This garment was seamless, woven in one piece from top to bottom.

'Let's not tear it,' they said to one another. 'Let's decide by lot who will get it.'

This happened that the Scripture might be fulfilled which said,

'They divided my garments among them and cast lots for my clothing.'

So this is what the soldiers did.

Near the cross of Jesus stood his mother, his mother's sister, Mary the wife of Clopas, and Mary of Magdala. When Jesus saw his mother there, and the disciple whom he loved standing near by, he said to his mother, 'Dear woman, here is your son,' and to the disciple, 'Here is your mother.' From that time on, this disciple took her into his home.

THE DEATH OF JESUS
Later, knowing that all was now completed, and so that the Scripture would be fulfilled, Jesus said, 'I am thirsty.' A jar of wine vinegar was there, so they soaked a sponge in it, put the sponge on a stalk of the hyssop plant, and lifted it to Jesus' lips. When he had received the drink, Jesus said, 'It is finished.' With that, he bowed his head and gave up his spirit.
John 19:16–30

The Church of the Holy Sepulchre, Jerusalem, at sunset. There is good evidence to support the traditional belief that the crucifixion took place on this site.

Inset: A wooden cross is carried in the Good Friday procession to the Church of the Holy Sepulchre, Jerusalem.

Morning has Broken

This joyful Eastertide,
  Away with sin and sorrow.
My Love, the Crucified,
  Hath sprung to life this morrow.

Had Christ that once was slain,
  Ne'er burst his three-day prison,
Our faith had been in vain:
  But now hath Christ arisen.

My flesh in hope shall rest,
  And for a season slumber:
Till trump from east to west
  Shall wake the dead in number.

Jerusalem at dawn, from the Mount of Olives. In the foreground is the distinctive church of Dominus Flevit ('Jesus wept'); beyond, the walls of the old city and the Rockefeller Museum.

Death's flood hath lost his chill,
    Since Jesus crossed the river:
Lover of souls, from ill
    My passing soul deliver.

G.R. Woodward

The Empty Tomb

The Garden Tomb, Jerusalem, a beautifully kept haven amidst the noise and bustle of East Jerusalem.

An ancient tomb with a rolling stone at the entrance, Jerusalem.

Early on the first day of the week, while it was still dark, Mary of Magdala went to the tomb and saw that the stone had been removed from the entrance. So she came running to Simon Peter and the other disciple, the one Jesus loved, and said, 'They have taken the Lord out of the tomb, and we don't know where they have put him!'

So Peter and the other disciple started for the tomb. Both were running, but the other disciple outran Peter and reached the tomb first. He bent over and looked in at the strips of linen lying there but did not go in. Then Simon Peter, who was behind him, arrived and went into the tomb. He saw the strips of linen lying there, as well as the burial cloth that had been around Jesus' head. The cloth was folded up by itself, separate from the linen. Finally the other disciple, who had reached the tomb first, also went inside. He saw and believed. (They still did not understand from Scripture that Jesus had to rise from the dead.)
John 20:1–9

The Road to Emmaus

The Sea of Galilee soon after sunrise.

Now that same day two of them were going to a village called Emmaus, about seven miles from Jerusalem. They were talking with each other about everything that had happened. As they talked and discussed these things with each other, Jesus himself came up and walked along with them; but they were kept from recognising him.
Luke 24: 13–16

Afterwards Jesus appeared again to his disciples by the Sea of Tiberias (right). It happened this way: Simon Peter, Thomas (called Didymus), Nathanael from Cana in Galilee, the sons of Zebedee, and two other disciples were together. 'I'm going out to fish,' Simon Peter told them, and they said, 'We'll go with you.' So they went out and got into the boat, but that night they caught nothing.

Early in the morning, Jesus stood on the shore, but the disciples did not realise that it was Jesus.
John 21: 1–4

The Ascension

When he had led them out to the vicinity of Bethany, he lifted up his hands and blessed them. While he was blessing them, he left them and was taken up into heaven. Then they worshipped him and returned to Jerusalem with great joy. And they stayed continually at the temple, praising God.
Luke 24: 50—53

The Mount of Olives. The church with the distinctive onion-shaped domes is the Church of Mary Magdalene, built by Czar Alexander III in 1888. The old city of Jerusalem and the Dome of the Rock lie beyond.

Index

A

Annunciation, Church of the 18–19
Ascension 62–63

B

Banias 38
Bar-Mitzvah 20
Bartimaeus 45
Beatitudes, Mount of the 30–31
Bethany 46–47
Bethlehem 10–17
Bethsaida 28

C

Caesarea Phillippi 38
Capernaum 28–29
Crucifixion 54–55

D

Damascus Gate 20
Dome of the Rock 48–50
Dominus Flevit church 56–57

E

Emmaus road 61

F

farmers 36–37
fishermen 26–27

G

Galilee, Sea of 26–27
Garden Tomb 58–59
Gethsemane 48–49, 52–53
Good Friday procession 55

H

Hermon, Mount 38–39
Holy Sepulchre, Church of the 54–55

J

Jericho 25, 44–45
Jerusalem 48–59
Damascus Gate 20
Western Wall 20
John the Baptist 9, 22–23
Jordan, River 22–23

L

Lazarus 46
loaves and fishes, miracle of the 32–33

M

Mary Magdalene, Church of 62–63
Miracle of the Loaves and Fishes, Church of the 33

N

Nativity, Church of the 14
Nazareth 18
Negev desert 9

O

olive trees 52
Olives, Mount of 48–49, 62–63

P

Palm Sunday procession 51
Peter 28
Primacy, Church of the 32–33

R

Rockefeller Museum 56–57

S

St Peter in Gallicantu 52–53
Samaritan woman 43
shepherds 11, 34–35
sower, parable of the 36
synagogue, Capernaum 28–29

T

Temple Mount 48–49
Tabgha 32–33
Tabor, Mount 40–41
Temptation, Mount of the 25
tombs 58–59
Transfiguration 40–41

W

well, woman at the 43
Western Wall 20, 48–49
wilderness 9, 24-25

Acknowledgements

Scripture quotations in this publication, except pp. 9, 10, 34, are from the Holy Bible, New International Version. Copyright © 1973, 1978, 1984 International Bible Society. Published by Hodder & Stoughton.

All text is extracted from *A People's Life of Christ* by J.Paterson Smyth, unless otherwise indicated, and is reproduced by permission of Hodder & Stoughton Ltd.

Extract from *Eight Days in Israel* by E.M.Blaiklock (Ark Publishing, 1980). © Scripture Union, 130 City Road, London, EC1V 2NJ. Used by permission.

Extract from *The Historical Geography of the Holy Land*, by George Adam Smith by kind permission of the Executors of the late Lord Balerno.

All photographs are by Sonia Halliday and Laura Lushington except for those on pp. 20 (bottom), 35, 55 (Barry Searle); pp. 40, 51 (Jane Taylor); p. 15 (Barbara Warley).

Map by Richard Scott.